AF480613

Colton the Baby Polar Bear: Adventures in the Arctic, Copyright © 2019. All rights reserved related to written material, design, and image illustrations. No part of this work covered by the copyright herein may be reproduced or used in any form or by any means, graphic, electronic or mechanical without the prior written permission of Real Peoples History, Zig Misiak. Any request for photocopying, recording, taping or information storage and retrieval systems of any part of this book shall be directed in writing to Real Peoples History.

Zig Misiak: Author   Jennifer Bettio: Illustrator
Contributor: Raymond R. Skye, Tuscarora/Seneca, Grand River Six Nations Territory
Educational consultant: Shaylyn Misiak, ECE, BEd, BA (hons.), OCT
Revised 2022, ISBN 9798844343728

Other publications by Zig Misiak

FIRST NATIONS RESOURCE COLLECTION, ISBN 978-0-9811880-2-7
WAMPUM: The Story of Shaylyn the Clam, ISBN-978-0-9811880-8-9
WAR of 1812: Highlighting Native Nations, ISBN 978-0-9811880-5-8
WAR of 1812: Western Hooves of Thunder, ISBN 978-0-9811880-3-4
TONTO: The Man in Front of the Mask, ISBN 978-0-9811880-6-5
4 in 1 LEARNING: French & English, ISBN 978-0-9950128-0-6
ABC's Colouring Book, ISBN 978-0-9950128-9-9
1-2-3's, Shapes & Colours Colouring Book, ISBN 978-1-7771417-0-7
ASHER: of the Heron Clan, ISBN 978-0-9950128-3-7
COLTON: of the Bear Clan, ISBN 978-8-9950128-2-0
CRISTINE: of the Snipe Clan, ISBN 978-0-9950128-7-5
DARYL: of the Deer Clan, ISBN 978-0-9950128-6-8
LUKE: of the Eel Clan, ISBN 978-1-7771417-7-6
MEAGHAN: of the Hawk Clan, ISBN 978-0-9950128-8-2
RYAN: of the Wolf Clan, ISBN 978-0-9950128-5-1
STANLEY: of the Beaver Clan, ISBN 978-1-7771417-8-3
TYLER: of the Turtle Clan, ISBN 978-0-9950128-1-3
POLISH Heritage Guide, ISBN 978-1-7771417-5-2

www.canadianauthoreducation.com

About Clans

All **First Nations, Métis and Inuit People**, similar to other nations around the world, have a family system. The First Nations Métis, and Inuit people are interwoven with nature like interdependent fibres in the colourful and mysterious tapestry of life.

Clans existed well before Europeans came to **Turtle Island,** known to many as North America. In the case of the **Haudenosaunee**, also known as the Six Nations or Iroquois, they even existed before the coming of the **Peacemaker**.

The BEAR, the main story in this book, is one of the nine (9) Clan animals of the Six Nations. These two introductory pages, plus the supplemental pages at the end of the story, will be informative.

Relax and get ready to enjoy the bear's adventures in the Arctic as well as becoming enlightened about First Nations Clans.

9 Clans of the Haudenosaunee

Of the land	Bear	Wolf	Deer
Of the water	Eel	Beaver	Turtle
Of the air	Heron	Snipe	Hawk

Other examples of First Nations animals and relations.

West Coast Haida
They belong to one of two groups of Clans, the Eagle or the Raven.

Anishinaabe Clans
Bear, Otter, Fish, Eagle, Loon, Crane, Deer.

Mikmaq Spirit Animals
Bear, Lynx, Beaver, Crow, Eagle, Fox, Moose, Wolf.

The Young Man and the Clans

The **Young Man** noticed that there was a lack of support between people, especially when they were grieving. He spoke to the elders saying that all of nature worked in harmony and that humans needed to get back into that harmonious natural rhythm.

He was permitted to unfold his plan. First he had all the elder women of each family find and observe an animal they were drawn too. Over some time the women came back to him with their choices. He assigned those particular animals to each unit giving them that animals name.

He then had all the people gather at the river. There he divided them into two predetermined groups having one half cross to the other side.

Once everyone was settled in, the Young Man explained that the river was like the fire in their lodges that divided the mothers and father sides of the family.

He said, "Let the fire symbolize the division the river created. Let the Clans support and address each other across the fire in the longhouses. During loss the related Clans on the opposite side will console and lend assistance to those in grief."

The **Matriarchal** Clan system was born and created a strong bond amongst the Original Ones, the **Onkwehon:we**, becoming an important part of their lives, then and now.

The Young Man's concept of bringing the people together, as extended families, served them well. They worked together and continued to learn from nature, caring for it as the **Creator** had intended.

The Peacemaker

Sadly, when the Peacemaker arrived, years later, the Clan system was dysfunctional due to constant warfare between the nations. The Peacemaker, a woman named **Jikonsaseh** and **Hayenwah:tha**, re-established the Clans creating a strong foundation for their newly organized **Confederacy** based on the **Great Law of Peace**. He told the Onkwehon:we that from now on they would also be known as the Haudenosaunee, the People Building a Longhouse.

The Stories of Creation, formation of the Clans, the coming of the Peacemaker leading to the existence of the Confederacy are all available in detail in the Six Nations Iroquois Program Teachers Resource Guide . Written by Raymond R. Skye, Tuscarora/Seneca, and collaborators, from the Grand River Six Nations Territory and related Six Nations communities.

Colton Alonzo Misiak
Our Grandson

It was a cold **Arctic** December and mama **polar bear** had her big white furry arms curled gently around her two young **pups.** Colton and his sister had dark eyes, black noses and a touch of black on the tips of their ears. They were already covered in a fluffy white fur coat.

Mama built her den a long time ago by digging into a snow bank. She lived there alone and it protected her from the harsh Arctic weather. Now it's protecting all three of them.

The view through the dens entrance was beautiful. Under the clear blue sky the sun's rays made the snow sparkle. Green trees were scattered among the rolling white snow dunes.

Not far away from their den, crystal clear water wrapped itself around countless sheets of broken ice. The Arctic Ocean was always changing. Bluish-white mystical castle-like icebergs contrasted with the dark, but clear, blue water on which they majestically floated.

The pups depended on their mother for milk every day. Mama bear left her den often, sometimes followed by her pups, to find food. She needed to eat to create more milk. By closely watching their mother the pups were learning about their environment.

Polar bears are excellent hunters, very fast runners, and great swimmers. They are mostly white and are very hard to see in the snow. A perfect natural camouflage.

Colton and his sister played just outside their cave where their mother could watch them. They liked to wrestle and tumble over one another as they ran and rolled down the snow covered hills. The snow clung to their fur and sometimes they looked like large snow balls.

After playing, which always made them tired, they slowly waddled back to their den. There they ate and then laid down, curled up near their mother, and rested for a while.

The next day Colton woke up earlier than his mother and sister. He looked toward the opening of the den and slowly and quietly crept to the entrance. He sat and stared outside.

He glanced to his left, then to his right and then straight ahead. Suddenly he sprang to his feet and started to run as fast as he could toward a large hill. When he got to the top he found himself looking over a wide expanse of pure white ice floating on the water.

He allowed himself to slip downhill on his butt and all four paws. Nearing the bottom he had to dig in hard into the snow with his feet to stop from sliding into the icy water. He came to a screeching halt just in time.

Looking up he saw two young **Inuit** coming his way in a **kayak**. They wore traditional fur and hide clothes. They were focused and stared deeply into the water. They were **spear-fishing**.

The two young Inuit, one boy and one girl, noticed Colton peaking over a snow drift. The young girl waived to Colton and the boy gave him a warm smile.

Colton watched as they caught a big fish. They pulled it onto their kayak and strapped it to the top. They picked up their paddles and started to turn away from the icy shore line.

They made no sound as their kayak glided effortlessly over the surface of the blue water. They skillfully maneuvered between the ice-sheets and away from Colton.

The young girl, in the back of the kayak, looked over her shoulder and once again she waived at Colton before they finally disappeared into the distance, behind a small iceberg.

Colton heard a rustling sound behind him. Naturally sensitive to danger, he crouched then slowly and carefully looked all around him. Almost invisible, because it was all white, he saw a small creature with long ears. Colton quickly leapt toward it before it could run away.

They came face to face and looked into each others big black eyes. The long-eared animal came closer and twitched its nose. Colton tried to twitch his nose but he could not twitch.

Colton had just met an **Arctic hare.** Not only was the hare able to walk like Colton but it could hop. It had very powerful back legs that were much longer than its front ones.

Colton laid down and placed his head comfortably on his own paws. He wanted to watch the hare, his new friend. Suddenly, scaring Colton, the hare sprang up and jumped to its right. It quickly hopped away zig-zagging on top of the fluffy snow disappearing over a small hill.

Colton walked away noticing a hole in the ice with water in it. He put his head down and stared. A white head popped out of the water. Quickly it disappeared then it popped up again. Colton leaned forward and, gently, without fear they both touched noses.

Colton had just met a baby **seal.** The seal had never seen a polar bear before. The seal blinked and then smoothly, with hardly a ripple, slid under the water. It did not come back.

Continuing his journey Colton saw a small sheet of ice floating nearby. He leapt on it. The sheet of ice bobbled a bit but stayed afloat. Colton, lazily drifting along, soon found himself moving closer to two animals that looked much like the seal he met earlier, yet different.

The two **walruses** were quite big and were dark in colour. One of them had long teeth called **tusks**. They were lying near the edge of the water sunbathing. Colton's raft drifted away.

As Colton cruised along he stuck his head underwater. He saw a school of salmon. He dove in trying to catch one. He was not yet the hunter he needed to be and missed them all.

Colton was startled when he saw a huge black and white shadow approach him. It was much bigger than Colton. It was catching lots of salmon. Salmon were among the favorite foods of baby **orcas**. The orca looked at Colton with smiling eyes and slowly swam away.

Colton had to come up for fresh air. As he swam to the surface he opened his mouth and accidentally caught a small salmon. He climbed out of the water and started to walk toward another hole where he spotted a strange looking fish called a **narwhal.**

Colton gasped and his mouth opened. The salmon fell into the water. The narwhal dove underwater and caught the salmon. He thanked Colton as he thought it was a gift from him.

The narwhal gracefully dove forward and disappeared underwater. Colton decided to move further inland. He noticed that not everything was completely covered in snow.

The Arctic had short summers during which assorted plants grew. Here and there clusters of beautiful flowers bloomed, including, among the rocks, the Arctic poppy.

Colton also saw dwarf trees, moss, and hardy patches of grass. All of this vegetation was being used in various ways by the animals that lived there.

Colton began to climb up a low rocky hill when he heard a soft, hoot, hoot. He looked up and there, slightly above him, was a very small cute animal, mostly white, but with dark spots and stripes in its wings. He noticed that it only had two legs.

The little creature, with big round eyes and a tiny orange beak, was a **snowy owl.** She only needed two legs because she also had wings meaning that she could fly.

Before Colton could get any closer to the baby snow owl she spread her wings and sprung into the air. With her large wings slowly flapping, she rose higher into the sky.

As she faded into the distance she made a small circle back toward Colton giving one more hoot. She turned around again and in minutes became nothing more than just a speck.

Colton was pleased that he was meeting all kinds of creatures that shared the Arctic with him. It looked quite barren yet it was very much full of life.

Colton walked for quite some time without seeing any more animals. He moved his head searching to the left, to the right, up into the sky and down toward the ground.

As Colton walked around a small rocky and snow covered hill he heard another strange sound. He moved closer to where he thought the sound was coming from. There he saw an animal that, for the first time, looked much the same as he did.

When it saw Colton it made a little snorting sounds coming from its nose and with one of its front hooves it scraped the snow. It appeared to be a little frightened but did not need to be.

This young **caribou** was a bit taller than Colton with longer legs and its fur was a chocolate brown colour. Colton also noticed tiny bumps on its head near its ears. These bumps were antlers in the process of growing. Someday they will grow to be much bigger.

After greeting one another, with a touch of their noses, the little caribou turned away from Colton and with its gangly legs trotted very playfully toward a hill. Colton followed. As the caribou disappeared down the other side Colton peered over the hill and there he saw thousands of other caribou. It was a very large herd on the move.

Colton watched as the little caribou blended in with the herd and started to move along with them. The caribou were migrating, meaning that they moved seasonally from one place to another looking for better grazing grounds and safe places to deliver their babies.

Colton was having lots of fun. He met new friends that lived in the Arctic. He saw animals that flew, animals that lived under water and those that lived on the snow and land.

By now Colton was getting a bit hungry as the day was coming to an end. He felt that it was best to find his way back home. Colton started to walk a little faster yet he still found time to purposely and playfully tumble down some small snow covered hills.

Colton was quite smart and after turning himself around he began to walk back in the direction from where he came. He followed his old footprints and was retracing his steps.

Little Colton was lucky not having met animals that were dangerous. He had to be very careful because he was alone and still a small bear that did not know how to protect itself.

Colton heard a new sound. It was yelping. He immediately stopped in his tracks. When he looked to his left he saw two animals playing around some rocks. These **Arctic foxes** looked even more like him than any of the other animals he had seen before.

Colton eagerly pranced over to them. These baby Arctic foxes were white with long fur like Colton's. They had ears and four legs as well. The difference was that their tails and legs were longer than Colton's but Colton was still bigger and heavier.

Colton, knowing that he had to get home quickly, did not stop as he walked between them. The Arctic foxes continued playing and only casually glanced at Colton as he passed by.

Throughout Colton's entire journey a **bald eagle,** soaring high in the sky, was watching him. The eagle had never seen a baby polar bear as curious as Colton. As the day went on the eagle grew fonder of Colton and became his protector even though Colton did not know it.

Colton climbed his last snow hill for the day. From there he saw his mother and sister in the distance. They were on their hind legs looking toward him. He knew they must have been worried but now they were very happy to see Colton. He was also very happy to be home.

Mama bear and her two young cubs were together again. Soon they would be **hibernating**.

The winters in the Arctic are long, very cold and dark. The den would protect them. All three of them ate well and they had plenty of stored fat to keep them healthy until the spring.

Mama bear had taught her cubs how to survive. In the coming spring Colton and his sister would venture out by themselves, make a den and someday have their own family.

Arctic Circle
RUSSIA
FINLAND
SWEDEN
NORWAY
Arctic Regions
North Pole +
ARCTIC OCEAN
ICELAND
Greenland
(Denmark)
Alaska
(U.S.)
CANADA

Key Vocabulary

Arctic: Comes from the Greek word 'arktikos' meaning 'near the bear'. Parts of the Yukon, Northwest Territories, Nunavut and Northern Quebec are located within the Arctic Circle.

Arctic fox: Is also known as the white fox, polar fox, or snow fox .

Arctic hare: It survives in the winter by adding fat to its body and its fur turns white.

Bald eagle: They live in the Arctic during summer months. Young eagles are called eaglets.

Caribou: Caribou and reindeer belong to the same species. Caribou are larger and mostly live in the wild.

Clans: Traditionally, not always, Clans are a group of people related by a blood-line. Usually, in this part of the world, through the women. For example, in the Haudenosaunee culture an individual would have their own personal name, belonging to the Wolf Clan of the Mohawk Nation.

Confederacy: The union of the original Five Nations under the Great Law of Peace as composed and implemented by the Peacemaker, Hayenwah:tha and Jikonsaseh. It re-established the Clan system and the Nations councils.

Creator: As it is with many other nations around the world there is a Creator of all things. All First Nations, Inuit and Métis have a Creator in their stories related to the 'Beginning Times'.

First Nations, Métis and Inuit People: First Nations were once referred to as 'Indians' in Canada and still are in the United States. First Nations are the 'Original People' from this part of the world. The Métis are people of mixed blood, First Nations and Euro-American. Inuit, living in northern Canada, parts of Greenland and Alaska, are not First Nations but are also 'Original People'. Indigenous, Aboriginal and Native are all words that are used interchangeably when referring to the three groupings of people. The word 'Indian' is more acceptable when used in a historic context.

Grazing: This is when caribou, just like cows, feed on the plants and grass in fields.

Great Law of Peace: It is an actual living and breathing oral, then later written, document outlining guidelines where reason, moderation and careful discussion were informed and influenced by past events, the current situation, and the possible impact on seven generations into the future. (www.canadianauthoreducation.com)

Harp seal: They can hold their breath underwater for up to 20 minutes.

Haudenosaunee: In the Onondaga language this means the People of the Longhouse or the Longhouse Builders. The original Five Nations Confederacy, consisted of the Mohawk, Seneca, Onondaga, Oneida and Cayuga People.

Key Vocabulary

Hayenwah:tha: He was born Onondaga. He suffered greatly before coming into contact with the Peacemaker. He was crucial in assisting the Peacemaker with spreading the peace among the nations and establishing the 'Great Law of Peace'.

Hibernate: This is when animals go into a deeper than normal sleep in the winter. Each animal is different.

Jikonsaseh: The Peacemaker converted her from evil and she then became one of his biggest supporters spreading the 'Good Word'. She is sometimes referred to as the original Clan Mother.

Kayak: A boat, built for one or two, used for hunting and transportation. Traditionally made from wood and hide.

Matriarchal: A system based on female lineage wherein women had great influence, control and leadership in all aspects of a particular society.

Narwhal: The tusk/horn is used for sensing changes in the environment in which they live.

Onkwehon:we: In the Mohawk language this is translated as the 'Original People' or the 'First Ones'. Inuit also refer to themselves in this way.

Orca: Often referred to as a 'Killer Whale' they are members of the dolphin family.

Peacemaker: He was a Wyandot who, with the help of others, brought the original Five Nations of the Haudenosaunee together in peace. The Great Law of Peace evolved and the Haudenosaunee Confederacy was born.

Polar bear: Sleuth or pack are the terms used when referring to a group of polar bears. The worlds largest bear.

Pups: A seal, shark, dog, fox are some of the other animals that have their babies referred to as pups.

Snowy owl: Males are all white but females have black specs or stripes and different parts of their bodies.

Spear-fishing: This was a traditional way of fishing using a long stick with a bone pointed tip.

Turtle Island: In the Haudenosaunee creation story, a woman, Sky Woman, fell from the sky landing on a sea turtle. Over a long period of time many other land masses were formed on earth. North America is a part of Turtle Island.

Tusk: Are actually the upper teeth of a walrus. Used for climbing hills, defense and digging for food.

Walrus: Called pinnipeds for their fin-like flippers, just like seals. Males and females have tusks.

Young Man: Inspired by the Creator, this man presented a plan to his people from which the Clan system was born.

Bear Clan

Ohkwa:ri Ota:ra

Pronounced: Oh-gwah-ree-Odah-rah

Clan of the Earth

Disciplined, wise, of great moral character, devoted, courageous

People of the Bear Clan are devoted to their clan family, and stand firmly united in the welfare of their nationhood. They are great hunters and providers. Bear Clan people are considered to be wise teachers, and believe moral character is the basis for a strong community. They draw their strength from that principle which has served them well in life. The bear has a reputation of being fearless no matter what danger it may encounter. Centuries ago Iroquois warriors were said to be like the bear, noble, brave, and strong. They were taught to face danger with courage and dignity. This strength is still prevalent in the hearts of the Bear Clan people.

In oral teachings a story tells how the Bear Clan acquired knowledge of natural medicines. A long time ago one of its members was given instructions as to the healing properties of such medicines, and where they could be found. From that time on the Bear Clan became known as "healers." Their spiritual connection to nature keeps them aligned with the sacredness of all living things. The Bear Clan's presence is noted across all the Iroquois clans and nations.

Words by: Awedodyoh, Raymond R. Skye
Tuscarora * Seneca
Grand River Six Nations Territory
www.canadianauthoreducation.com

Questions & Answers

1. **What was the main purpose of the Clan?**

To create family units that would help one another through daily living but mainly for consoling during times of grief.

2. **Who played a key part in developing the Clans and how?**

The Young Man presented the idea first to the elders then he was allowed to speak to the people.

3. **How did the Clan animals help the people develop character?**

They were examples of co-operation and coexistence with nature.

4. **Who were the key players in the Clan structure and what roles did they play?**

The women, caretakers of life, watched and selected the animals they related to.

5. **How would Clan members take care of one another?**

Support one another every day. Help each other by sharing the necessities of life. Remind one another to be thankful to the Creator and observe the ceremonies.

6. **How did the Clan structure help build a sense of community?**

It created family relations that were obligated to help one another. Heron Clan helped Heron Clan within a particular nation but did not exclude interacting with other Clans in other nations.

7. **What do you think a person would do if they saw one of their Clan members being bullied or struggling to learn something?**

They would help them by trying to create a peaceful solution failing that by removing them from

	Hawk	Bear	Wolf	Turtle	Heron	Snipe	Deer	Beaver	Eel
Mohawk		X	X	X					
Seneca	X	X	X	X	X	X	X	X	
Oneida		X	X	X					
Onondaga	X	X	X	X	X	X	X	X	X
Cayuga		X	X	X	X	X			
Tuscarora		X	X	X		X	X	X	X

* Shaded area depicts the **Clans common** to all the Haudenosaunee (Six Nations) People

Can you identify the 9 Clan animals prints?

The 9 Clan animals prints identified.

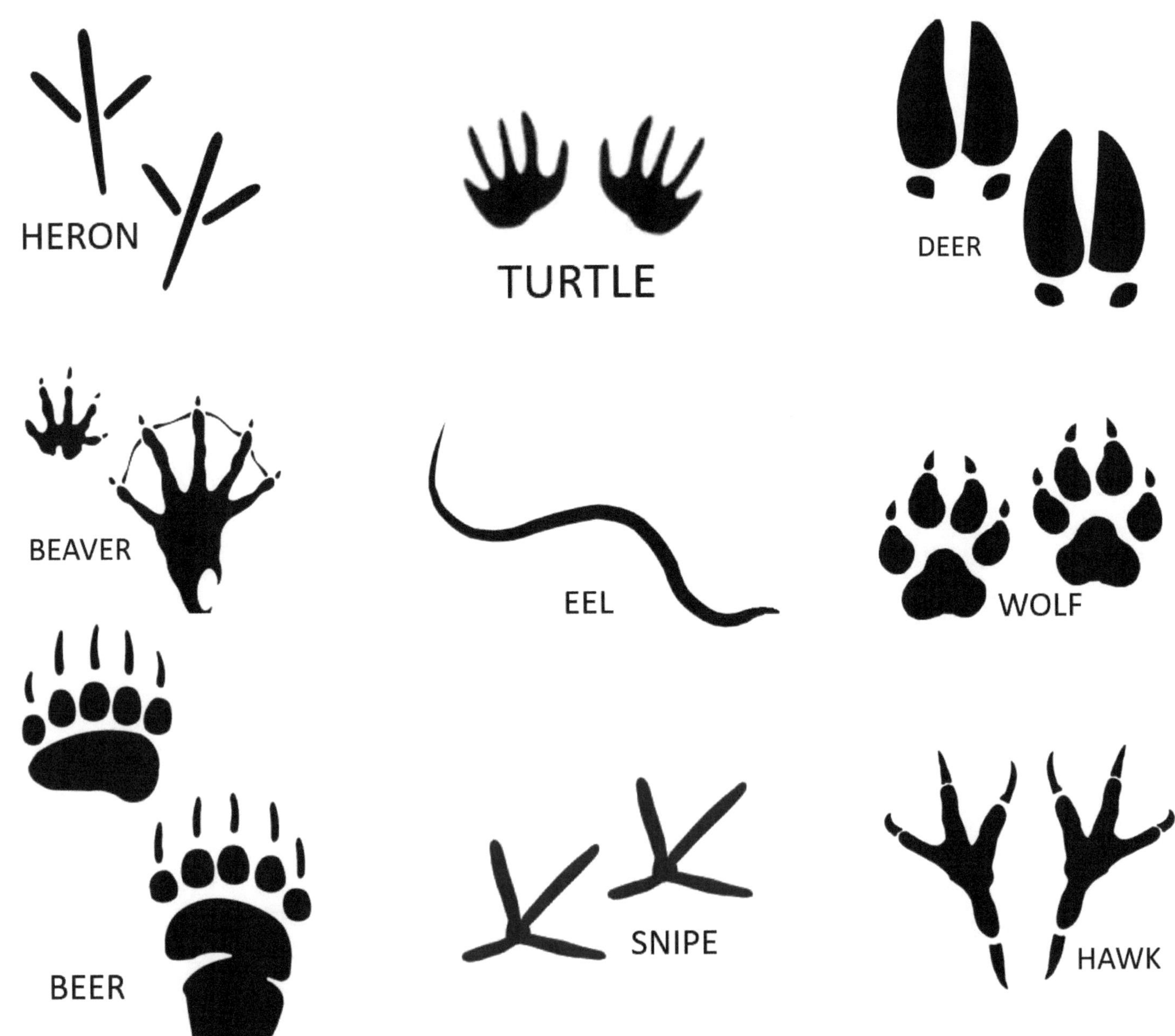

Colouring Activity

Artist's Name:

Zig Misiak is a highly respected, award-winning Canadian author of First Nations books and educational resources. As a child, often on his own, Zig became very curious about the children "across the bridge" at the nearby residential school in Brantford, Ontario. Then, as an adult, he embraced and cultivated interest and enduring relationships with his neighbours and friends, the Haudenosaunee, the Grand River Six Nations People.

Queen Elizabeth II Diamond Jubilee Medal
Sovereign's Medal
Lieutenant Governor's Ontario Heritage Award for Lifetime Achievement
Polish Army Gold Medal - 1st Degree
Canadian Polish Congress Award of Merit
Polish Combatants' Bronze Cross
Shining Star Award
George and Olive Seibel Award
Inductee: Ancaster High School Hall of Distinction
Canadian Aboriginal Veterans Association Medallion

As a child, often on his own, Zig became very curious about the children "across the bridge" at the nearby residential school in Brantford, Ontario. Then, as an adult, he embraced and cultivated interest and enduring relationships with his neighbours and friends, the Haudenosaunee, the Grand River Six Nations People. Zig Misiak, became a well-known historical re-enactor who has travelled thousands of miles across Eastern Canada and the United States, participating in the re-enacting of major historical events from the French and Indian Wars, American Revolution, to the War of 1812. He also served in the Canadian Army, Royal Hamilton Light Infantry.

He is now recognized as an authority and a legend for his knowledge, understanding, and commitment to authenticity, as well as the strong friendships he has developed. He has studied and travelled to the very places he has written about in his many books. Zig has a deep love and respect for Indigenous People, recognizing that in spite of the many difficult challenges they have faced, they have remained true to their treaties. As Zig says, **"We must know them."**

Jennifer Bettio, born and raised in Guelph Ontario, is an arts and photography graduate of Sheridan College. With support of her parents she pursued her interests in the arts field that has brought her great success. She does commissioned paintings, art, graphics and design, advertising, illustrations and unique photography. Her French Canadian Métis background, allows her to exhibit a unique First Nations/Métis style of art.

www.ingramcontent.com/pod-product-compliance
Lightning Source LLC
Chambersburg PA
CBHW042010110726

48006CB00004B/1030